Hidden Heroes of the Bible

D0994215

Clio Turner

Illustrated by Beccy Blake

**Many people in the Bible did wonderful
things for God. Some of these people are well
known. Some are *less* well known. This
book tells the stories of some of these
people.**

Scripture Union

By the same author:
Great Escapes Of The Bible

© Clio Turner 2000

First published 2000
Reprinted 2002

Scripture Union, 207–209 Queensway, Bletchley, Milton
Keynes, MK2 2EB, England.
Email: info@scriptureunion.org.uk
Website: www.scriptureunion.org.uk

ISBN 1 85999 434 2

British Library Cataloguing-in-Publication Data.
A catalogue record of this book is available from the British
Library.

Printed and bound in Great Britain by
Creative Print and Design (Wales) Ebbw Vale.

Scripture Union is an international Christian charity working
with churches in more than 130 countries, providing resources
to bring the good news about Jesus Christ to children, young
people and families and to encourage them to develop
spiritually through the bible and prayer.

As well as our network of volunteers, staff and associates
who run holidays, church-based events and school Christian
groups,we produce a wide range of publications and support
those who use our resources through training programmes.

Contents

These stories come from a part of the Bible called the Old Testament. That means they happened a very long time ago! They have been re-told in modern English for young readers. We hope that you enjoy them.

Chapter One

Miriam, the clever sister

Miriam's heart was thumping hard. She had never been out so late before and she was afraid. She ran behind her mother through the hot streets of the town where they lived. They were trying not to be seen.

Her mother squeezed Miriam's hand and they stopped. Then she looked down at the small bundle which she was carrying.

He's all right!

But will he still be all right when we put him in the basket?

"I don't know," said Miriam's mother, "but it's our only hope."

Miriam felt sick. She didn't want the Egyptians to kill her baby brother. They ran on through the darkness.

"One more street and we're there!" said Miriam's mother.

They turned a corner... Suddenly Miriam's mother pushed her back into the shadows.

The Egyptian man was coming closer all the time. Soon the light of his torch would be on them...

"Oh God, *please* help us," prayed Miriam.

And just at that moment, the man stopped. He was only a few steps from where Miriam was standing, but he didn't look up. Instead he turned and knocked on a door. Someone opened the door, and the sound of music filled the street. The Egyptian laughed and went inside. He slammed the door and the street went quiet again.

"Thank you, God!" said Miriam.

But all of a sudden, there was another sound...

The slamming door had woken their baby!

"Quick!" hissed Mum. "Run as fast as you can!"

Miriam did *not* need to be told twice.

It was some time later that Miriam and her mother arrived on the banks of the River Nile. They were both very out of breath, but at least they had left the town without being seen.

Miriam's mother took off her back an empty basket which she had been carrying. Then she opened up her bundle and looked at the baby. He was fast asleep.

Miriam's mother took the baby and kissed him. Then she wrapped him up and put him in the basket. The baby woke and started to cry, but for the first time ever, Miriam's mother didn't pick him up. Instead she pushed the basket into the reeds, made sure it was safe, and turned away.

"This is where the important people come to wash," she said. "Perhaps one of them will take pity on my son." And slowly, sadly, Miriam's mother went back home, leaving Miriam to watch over her little brother.

Miriam's people, the Israelites, were slaves. Their Egyptian masters were cruel and they didn't like the Israelites. Their ruler, the Pharaoh, even gave an order to kill all the slave baby boys! Miriam's mother had been very clever and had kept her baby safe for three months. But now, he was growing too big and too noisy to keep him a secret. She had to let him go.

Miriam hid in the reeds, trying to watch what happened to the baby. But after a while...

Miriam was woken by a great splash! She jumped to her feet. The basket had been pulled out of the water by a servant girl. An important-looking young woman stood beside her. It was Pharaoh's daughter – the Princess!

The Princess had made up her mind. "I want to keep him," she said. "All I need now is a servant who is good with babies, to do all the hard work!"

The Princess was so surprised, she didn't know what to say. So Miriam kept talking. She couldn't *believe* how brave she was being. "My mother's wonderful with children!" she said. "She'll look after this one for you, if you like!"

This is just what I want, thought the Princess. "I'll pay her well," she said.

"Perfect!" said Miriam.

So Miriam ran home with some amazing news. Miriam's mother was going to be paid to look after her own baby!

★ ★ ★

When the baby was old enough, he was taken to the palace and brought up as a royal prince. And when he grew up, God used him to rescue all Miriam's people out of slavery! He became very famous. His name was Moses.

But remember that if it wasn't for Miriam, *Moses'* story might never have been told.

If you want to know more about Miriam and Moses, their story begins in the book of Exodus, chapter 2.

Chapter Two

Deborah goes to war

Deborah was a very busy woman! She was a wife. She was a mother. And she was also the main leader of God's people, the Israelites. People trusted Deborah to hear God clearly. So they brought all their problems to Deborah. And even though Deborah was very busy, she did her best to sort out everybody's problems.

Whenever God's people had disagreements, they would go to Deborah. Deborah would know what to do. God made Deborah very wise, which was a big help to the Israelites.

But as you can see, Deborah had a very
full life!

Now, at that time the Israelites had an
enemy. They were an evil people called
the Canaanites. The Canaanites did not care
about right or wrong. Their king, Jabin of
Hazor, *always* thought he was right because
he was stronger than everybody else. He
had nine hundred chariots and a huge
army. If he wanted something, he just took

it. For twenty years he had taken everything he wanted from Israel. He had stolen people. He had stolen food. He had stolen land. The Israelites were desperate by the end of this time.

"God, please help us. Do something!" they cried. "The Canaanites are taking all we have!" God listened to his people's prayers and he gave Deborah a message. Deborah sent for Barak, the captain of Israel's army.

Deborah went on to explain. "God has said that he will bring the Canaanite army down to the river. Then your army will be able to run down the mountains and attack them."

But Barak was not as brave as Deborah had hoped.

"What?" said Deborah. She was quite shocked but she agreed to go with Barak.

But she said to Barak, "Because you would not go alone, God has told me that he will hand the leader of the Canaanite army over to a woman and not to you."

And so they went to war.

★ ★ ★

Barak gathered ten thousand soldiers together and they headed up to the mountains. As soon as the Canaanite army came to the foot of the mountains, Deborah cried out to Barak, "Go! Now is your moment! Remember God himself is on your side!"

So Barak charged down the mountain with his soldiers.

Then a most unusual thing happened. It started raining, *very* hard. Water seemed to run everywhere. The river burst its banks and began turning all the land around it into a muddy pool. And the Canaanite army – with all its great chariots – got stuck in the mud.

By the end of the day, not one Canaanite was left alive except Sisera, the Captain of their army. When he saw that the battle was going badly, Sisera left his chariot and ran. He didn't care what happened to his soldiers. He wanted only to escape himself. He ran a long way and then came to a tent owned by a woman called Jael. Many people lived in tents in those days.

But when Sisera came inside, he got more than he bargained for.

Jael told him to lie down and rest. Sisera went and hid himself under a blanket. Jael gave Sisera milk to drink and soon he was asleep. Jael picked up a tent-peg. She picked up a hammer. She went quietly to where Sisera was sleeping. Then...

Wham! With one hard hit Sisera was dead. Jael had been very brave and had killed him with a peg!

19

Barak arrived soon afterwards. He was trying to find where Sisera was hiding. Jael showed him the place where Sisera now lay dead.

"Well," said Barak, "God handed the leader of the Canaanite army over to a woman, just as he said he would."

And the land had peace for forty years after that.

Deborah and Barak were so pleased that they sang this song to tell of what God had done!

God always saves his people,
He's done it once again.
He's done it through the mud
And he's done it through the rain.

He even used a woman
To set his people free.
So never let me hear you say
That God cannot use me!

If you want to know more about Deborah, her story can be found in the book of Judges, chapters 4 and 5.

Chapter Three

Gideon, the most unlikely leader

Gideon was not a very big man. Gideon was not a very strong man. Gideon was certainly not a very *brave* man when God started talking to him. In fact, Gideon was very scared when an angel from God first visited him.

The lord is with you, mighty warrior.

"Who? Me?" said Gideon. "I'm not a mighty warrior."

"But you can be, with God," said the angel. "Go! God is sending you to save your people from the Midianites."

The Midianites were Israel's latest enemies. For seven years they had been attacking Israel and making life miserable.

"But... but... there must be some mistake," said Gideon. "I am the weakest in my family. And my family is the weakest in all Israel!"

"There is no mistake," said the angel. "It's not *your* power that's important. It's God's! God wants someone who will rely on him and not think he can do it on his own. It is very clear that you couldn't do much on your own!"

Spurred on by this, Gideon got together an army and went out to fight the Midianites.

Although he still felt weak and rather unsure of himself, Gideon was pleased that so many people joined him. He had thirty-two thousand men in his army.

"Who knows?" he thought to himself, "Perhaps even I can beat the Midianites with all these people on my side."

But God had other ideas.

God said, "Gideon, this army of yours is too large. If you win with this many people, you will think that it is because you are strong. You will not realise that it is because I am strong. I want you to tell all your men who are frightened to go home!"

Gideon didn't like the sound of this. After all, it was better to go into battle with scared soldiers than with no soldiers at all. But he did what God had said.

The result was even worse than he expected. More than twenty thousand men got up and left right away!

'What do I do now?' said Gideon.

"You must trust me some more!" said God.

Then God said, "Gideon, I want you to lose some *more* of your men. You still have too many. Take those that are left down to the water to drink. When they are there, I will tell you exactly which men you should take."

Gideon thought this was a very strange way of choosing an army. But he said to himself, "Choosing me as leader of the army was very strange too. God is full of surprises!"

So he took his men down to the river.

God said to Gideon, "Give me the men who bring the water to their mouths. The rest you can send home."

"What?" said Gideon. There were only three hundred men in the group which God had chosen!

"With these men, I will give you victory over the Midianites!" said God.

And he did. This is how it happened...

★ ★ ★

On God's orders, Gideon and his army waited until the middle of the night. They were going to give the Midianites a big surprise!

Then Gideon and his men crept to the edge of the enemy camp. Each man had in his hand a pottery jar containing a burning flare, and a trumpet.

Suddenly Gideon broke his pottery jar. There was a burst of flame. Then Gideon gave a loud blast on his trumpet. All the other men did the same. Then they yelled at the tops of their voices, "A sword for God and for Gideon!" The night air was filled with flames and the sound of voices.

The Midianites panicked. They turned on each other with their swords! It was easy for Gideon and his men to beat all the Midianite army.

Then with the help of other loyal men, Gideon and his army chased the Midianites right off Israel's land.

The land had peace again for forty years.

Who would have believed it? Gideon learned that when you work with God, all things are possible.

If you would like to know more about Gideon, his story can be found in the book of Judges, chapters 6,7 and 8.

Chapter Four

Ruth, the best friend in the world

Ruth lived with her mother-in-law, Naomi, and her sister-in-law, Orpah, in the country of Moab. Things had not been easy for them. First of all Naomi's husband had died. Then Ruth's husband died and then Orpah's husband died as well. All three women were left very lonely and very sad.

One day Naomi decided to go back to the country of Israel where she used to live. But Ruth loved Naomi and would not let her go.

Naomi had a strong will. But Ruth was even *more* determined than Naomi was. Ruth said to Naomi, "I want to take care of you and look after you. So don't ask me to go away. I will make my home in the place that is your home. And I will worship the God you worship in Israel!"

At last Naomi agreed to let Ruth go with her.

So the two women kissed Orpah goodbye and went on their way. Naomi decided to go back to the town where she used to live. It was called Bethlehem.

But when Naomi and Ruth arrived in Bethlehem things were harder than ever. They had so little money that some days there was not really enough food to eat.

It was the time of the barley harvest. Ruth said to Naomi, "I will go and see if I can find some barley lying in the fields. The farm workers often leave some behind."

"That's a good idea," said Naomi.

It was usual for poor people to be allowed to do this. So off Ruth went. Ruth went to a field that belonged to a man called Boaz. It was a hot day and Ruth worked very hard.

Boaz saw her in the afternoon and he asked someone who she was.

"She is the girl from Moab," said one of his workers. "She has come to Israel to help Naomi. And she's been doing a good job of it too. All day long she's been working away in the hot sun and I've only seen her take a rest once!"

Boaz was impressed! So he went over to speak to Ruth.

"I am Boaz, the owner of this field!" Boaz said. "I am also Naomi's distant relative."

Then Boaz said, "Ruth, I pray that God himself will reward you for what you have done."

"What do you mean?" said Ruth.

"God is always good to people who want to do right, Ruth," said Boaz. "You have left your own people and your country in order to look after an old woman. You have also come under the protection of the God of Israel! God himself has seen what you have done and he will reward you. "

When Ruth went home, she couldn't *wait* to tell Naomi all about Boaz! But it seemed as if Naomi already knew all about him.

"He's a very rich and very kind man," said Naomi. "You would do well to keep working in his field! He is also one of our relatives, so he will want to look after us."

So Ruth kept working in Boaz's fields, day after day. At last the barley harvest was finished. Ruth and Naomi had had plenty to eat for the last few weeks, but they were worried about the future.

"I have an idea," said Naomi. "And my idea is to do with Boaz."

Ruth blushed because she liked Boaz very much.

"Why don't you go down at the end of harvest party they are having tonight in Boaz's barn?" said Naomi. "After the party,

Boaz will sleep in the barn. If you lie down at his feet, Boaz will understand that you want to marry him!" This was the custom in those days.

Ruth blushed still more!

"I am quite sure that he will want to marry you too," said Naomi. You are a beautiful girl and you have a very kind heart!"

So Ruth followed her mother-in-law's advice. And it all turned out just as Naomi had said!

Ruth put on her best clothes and went to the barn where Boaz and his servants were having a party. After the party was finished, Boaz went to sleep in a corner of the barn.

Ruth followed him and lay down at his feet as Naomi had told her to do. She lay there for a long time...

Then in the middle of the night, Boaz woke up.

Boaz understood that Ruth was asking him if he would like to marry her! Boaz was very pleased because he already loved Ruth. He had fallen in love with her as he watched her working so hard in his fields.

Naomi had got it exactly right. Ruth loved Boaz and Boaz loved Ruth. Ruth loved Boaz because she knew that he was a strong, kind man who loved God.

So Ruth and Boaz married and they were very happy. They had plenty of food to eat and they made sure that Naomi had plenty to eat too.

Before long, Ruth and Boaz had a baby called Obed. So Naomi had a grandson to look after. That made Naomi *very* happy.

Many years later Obed also had a grandson. He was called David and he became the king of Israel.

If you want to find out more about Ruth, her story can be found in the book of Ruth.

These stories come from a part of the Bible called the New Testament. That means they happened around the time of Jesus, about 2000 years ago.

Chapter Five

The man who believed Jesus

Sometimes the sort of people who end up being heroes are not the ones that we would expect.

When Jesus was alive in Galilee, a man who was a Centurion came up to him one day. Centurions were important Roman soldiers who had been sent to Israel to keep charge of the Jews who lived there. Most Jewish people didn't like Romans very much because they were very hard. But this Roman was different.

As soon as Jesus came into town, the Centurion ran to see him.

It was almost impossible to see Jesus because of the crowd of people who surrounded him. There were people who wanted to hear what Jesus said, and people who wanted Jesus to heal them. Some people wanted Jesus to bless their children and some people just wanted to see what Jesus looked like. People were pushing and shoving to be near Jesus but the Centurion waited patiently for his turn to come. At last, he worked his way to the front of the queue.

Jesus stopped what he was doing and listened. The Centurion went on to tell his story.

"My servant boy is sick," he said. "I think he needs a miracle more than anyone. In fact I think he'll *die*. He's always been a good servant, sir. Please take pity on him."

Jesus looked into the Centurion's face.
It was kind and honest.

The crowd cheered. Everyone was
looking forward to seeing a really good
miracle.

But the Centurion seemed flustered.
"Please sir," he said, "that's not what I
meant. I asked you to heal my servant, not
to come to my house. I am not worthy to
let a man like you walk across my
doorstep."

The crowd began to murmur but the Centurion went on, "I am a man who is used to giving orders. And when I give an order to my troops, it is usually obeyed! Surely it is the same with you, sir. If you order this sickness to leave my servant – I know that it will go. No sickness can remain, where *you* are in charge. My servant will get better, even if you don't take another step towards my home."

The crowd went very quiet, but a few people giggled. "What a strange man," whispered one.

But Jesus looked pleased.

Do you really mean what you are saying?

"Yes," replied the Centurion.

Then Jesus spoke in a loud voice to the crowd. "This man is an outsider and not a Jew like us. But he has more faith in God than I have ever seen in Israel. In God's eyes he's a hero because he trusts in him!"

"Well done," said Jesus to the Centurion. "Your servant shall be healed from this very moment."

Jesus patted the Centurion on the back and then went on his way.

The Centurion hurried home. It was a hot journey through the dusty streets. Eventually he reached the place where he lived on the outskirts of town.

The Centurion was overjoyed!

He went inside and heard the whole story. His servant had started to get better at exactly the time that Jesus had said he would.

If you want to know more about the Centurion, his story can be found in Matthew, chapter 8.

Chapter Six

Philip and the important man

Philip was a follower of Jesus. After Jesus had gone back to heaven, an angel appeared to Philip.

So Philip got up and went!

A very important man from Ethiopia was travelling along that road. God's Holy Spirit said to Philip, "Run up to that chariot and stay near it!" so Philip did that.

The Ethiopian man happened to be reading a bit from the Bible! It was a bit that Philip knew. The Ethiopian was reading aloud. "He was killed unfairly, but he never complained. He was like a sheep, who was killed ... for other people's wrongs."

The Ethiopian went on, "I have come to Jerusalem to find out about God. But now I am on my way home and I am still not sure that I know much about him. Who is the man in the Bible writing about? Can you help me?"

Philip grinned. "Yes, I can help you," he said. "The man in the Bible is writing about Jesus!"

The Ethiopian invited Philip to get into his chariot with him. Then Philip started to explain more. He told him that Jesus was God's son who had been sent into the world.

Philip explained that Jesus had lived a wonderful life...

He explained that Jesus had died a terrible death...

Then he explained that Jesus had died to take the punishment for all the wrong things we had done, so that we could be forgiven by God!

After that, Philip explained how the Ethiopian could be forgiven by God and follow Jesus himself. The Ethiopian had shining eyes by the time Philip had finished speaking.

"That's exactly what I want!" he said. "In fact, I think that this is what I've been looking for all my life!"

Philip was pleased. Then they came to a small river. The Ethiopian asked the driver to stop the chariot and he got out.

"Why can't I be baptised now?" he said. "Look. There is plenty of water here!"

"All right," said Philip. Together they waded into the stream. Philip took hold of the Ethiopian firmly but gently. After that he dipped him in the water and pulled him up again.

After that the Ethiopian went home to his own country very happy. "Now I can tell people about Jesus myself," he said.

And God's Holy Spirit took Philip on somewhere else.

If you want to know more about Philip and the Ethiopian, their story can be found in the book of Acts, chapter 8.

Chapter Seven

Barnabas, the kind man

Barnabas was a very good man who lived at a time when many people were becoming followers of Jesus. They became the first church in Jerusalem. Barnabas and some others began selling things which they owned.

They gave the money to the church leaders. The church leaders gave the money to the poor people in the church.

Pretty soon, Barnabas became a church leader too.

One day a man called Paul came back to Jerusalem. All the church leaders had heard of Paul because he had been a very bad man. When he had lived in Jerusalem before, he had hated the church. He had even tried to get the followers of Jesus put in jail or killed.

When Paul came back, he wanted to join the church! The other church leaders did not want him. But Barnabas was different. Barnabas went to see Paul. He found out that Paul had actually become a follower of Jesus. Barnabas thought that this was great. He quickly took Paul to meet the other church leaders.

Barnabas and Paul became best friends and they started telling people about Jesus together.

Paul was very good at talking to people about Jesus. Barnabas was very good at looking after people and loving them. Together they made a great team.

One day, Barnabas and Paul were telling people about Jesus in a place called Lystra. It was a long way from Jerusalem and the people who were living there didn't know much about God.

Paul saw a man who could not walk sitting in the crowd and he healed him in Jesus' name.

The people in Lystra were completely
amazed. They had never seen a miracle
before. But they did not realise that it was
Jesus' power that made the man walk.
Instead they thought Paul and Barnabas
had done it on their own.

"This is dreadful," said Paul to Barnabas. "What shall we do? They haven't listened to a word we've said about Jesus."

"Leave it to me," said Barnabas, "I want to try something."

In those days, tearing your clothes meant that you were very sad about something or very sorry about something.

The crowd were most surprised. "Why are the gods tearing their clothes?" they asked.

"Barnabas and I are not gods!" said Paul. "There is only *one* God in heaven."

Some people in the crowd started frowning. They had worshipped many gods for many years and they didn't like the thought that they could be wrong.

But Barnabas kept whispering in Paul's ear and encouraging him. "Well done Paul," he said. "Keep it up!"

Paul tried again. "The real God of heaven has sent us here so that we can tell you about his son Jesus." he said.

The crowd was listening now.

Paul said, "It is because we are followers of Jesus that God gave us the power to heal the man who could not walk. God loves all the people of the world. But he wants you to get to know him better. You can see that God is at work in the sunshine and the rain that make your crops grow. But God wants you to know that the best thing he *ever* did for you was to send you his own son Jesus. He took the punishment for all the things you have done wrong by dying on the cross."

"That was great, Paul," said Barnabas. But the crowd was not looking pleased. Many people in Lystra didn't like to hear that they had done wrong things. It made them angry to think that they had to ask God to forgive them.

But the crowd was not listening. Before long, a riot started. Paul and Barnabas almost got killed!

God rescued them.

But that's another story!

Barnabas and Paul continued on their way, telling people in other towns and cities all about Jesus. They travelled many miles together. Many people became followers of Jesus because of them.

Paul became one of the most famous followers of Jesus that the world has ever known. He wrote a lot of the Bible. He is sometimes called 'the apostle Paul' today.

But what would have happened if Barnabas hadn't been kind to Paul in the first place?

If you want to know more about Barnabas, his story can be found in Acts chapters 4, 9 and 14.

Some more books to enjoy!

Great Escapes of the Bible
Clio Turner

Many people in the
Bible had to escape
from danger for one
reason or another.
Rahab helped two spies
to escape from Jericho;
King David escaped being killled by
climbing out of a back window in his
house; an angel rescued Peter from prison.
These are just some of the exciting stories
in this new book.

ISBN 1 85999 433 4
Price £3.50

Bernard Bunting
The Missing Birthday
Ro Willoughby

Bernard's birthday
seems to have been
forgotten in the
excitement of preparing
for Christmas — or so
Bernard thinks. Does
God know about this
and does he care?
Bernard is in for a big
surprise.

ISBN 1 85999 327 3
Price £3.50

**Available from your local Christian bookshop, or
online at www.scriptureunion.org.uk/publishing
or call Mail Order direct on 01908 856006**